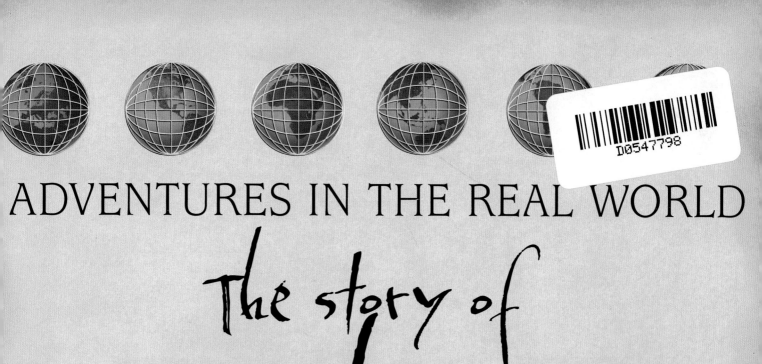

ADVENTURES IN THE REAL WORLD

The story of Explorers and Exploration

Penny Clarke

BOOK HOUSE

1 3 5 7 9 8 6 4 2

Published in Great Britain in 2007 by
Book House, an imprint of
The Salariya Book Company Ltd
25 Marlborough Place, Brighton BN1 1UB
www.salariya.com
www.book-house.co.uk

$ALARIYA

A CIP catalogue record for this book is available
from the British Library.

Printed and bound in China.
Printed on paper from sustainable sources.

Author: Penny Clarke
Illustrators: David Antram
Mark Bergin
Mark Peppé
Carolyn Scrace
Gerald Wood
Consultant: Timothy Akers
Editor: Stephen Haynes
Editorial Assistants: Mark Williams,
Rob Walker

Penny Clarke is an author and editor
specialising in children's information books.
She lives in Norfolk, England.

Timothy Akers studied at the universities of
Bradford and Hull, England. He is a maritime
archaeologist, specialising in new imaging
technology to locate archaeological remains both
underground and beneath the sea. He is a director
of the Underwater Heritage Trust, and is an
independent maritime research
archaeologist to the National Maritime
Museum, Greenwich, London.

The world is a book,
and those who do not
travel read only a page

HB ISBN-13: 978-1-905638-02-4
PB ISBN-13:.978-1-905638-03-1

Contents

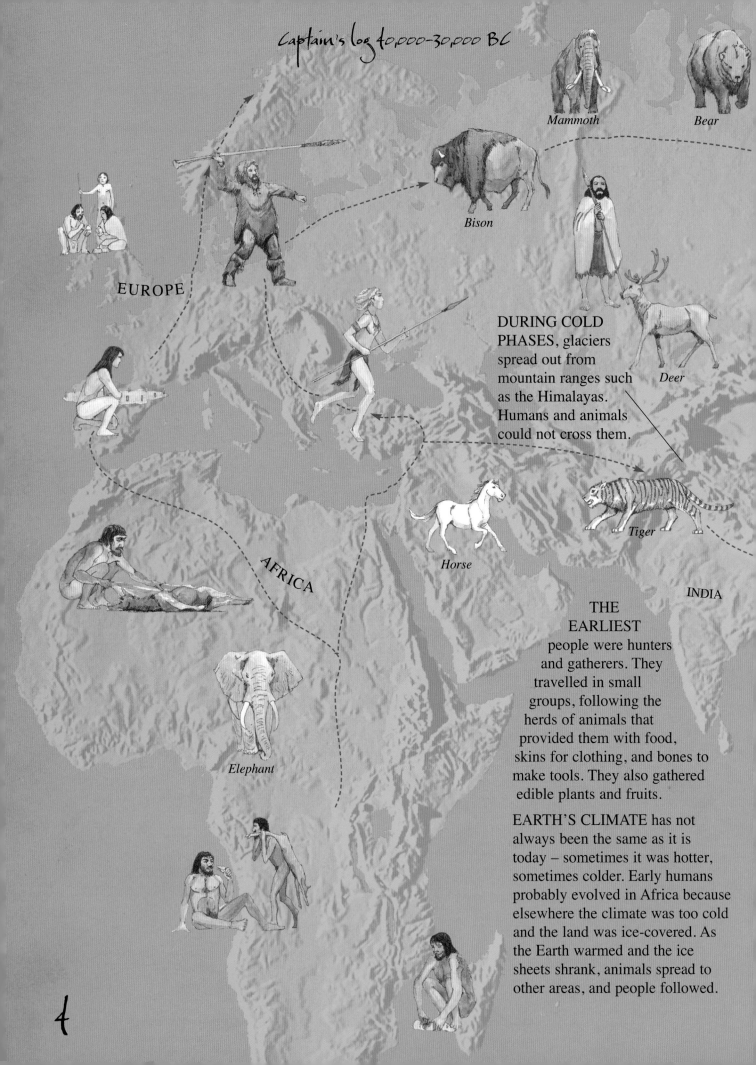

Mammoth

Bear

Bison

Deer

DURING COLD PHASES, glaciers spread out from mountain ranges such as the Himalayas. Humans and animals could not cross them.

EUROPE

Horse

Tiger

AFRICA

INDIA

Elephant

THE EARLIEST people were hunters and gatherers. They travelled in small groups, following the herds of animals that provided them with food, skins for clothing, and bones to make tools. They also gathered edible plants and fruits.

EARTH'S CLIMATE has not always been the same as it is today – sometimes it was hotter, sometimes colder. Early humans probably evolved in Africa because elsewhere the climate was too cold and the land was ice-covered. As the Earth warmed and the ice sheets shrank, animals spread to other areas, and people followed.

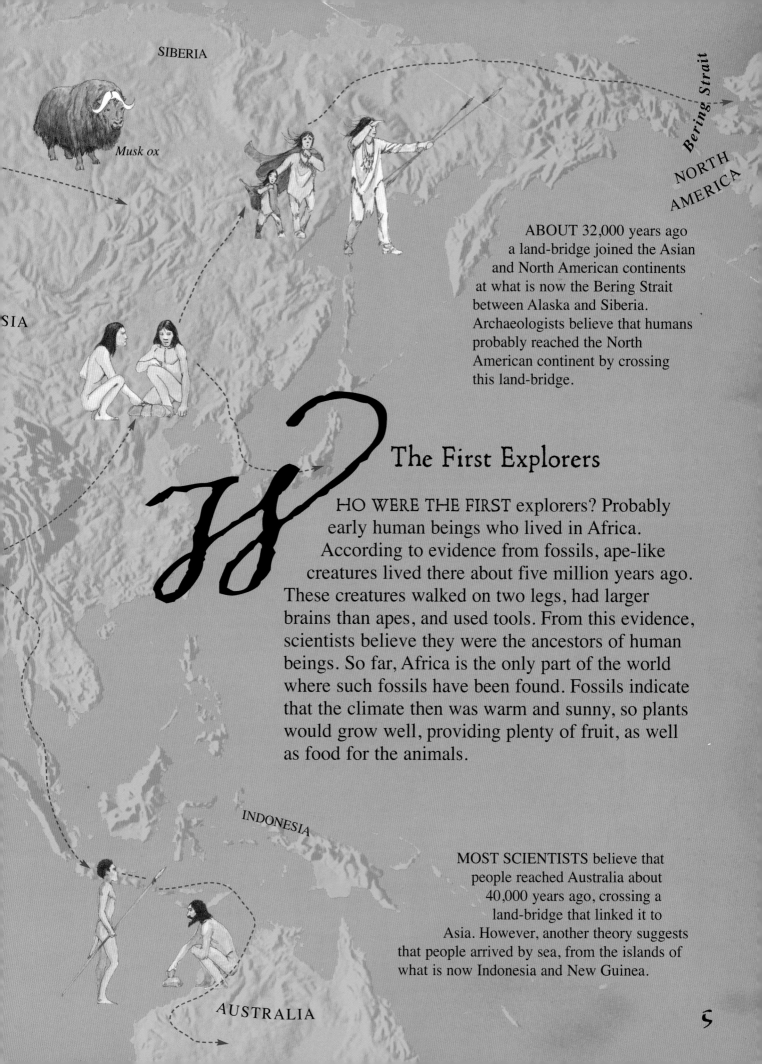

SIBERIA

Musk ox

SIA

Bering Strait

NORTH AMERICA

ABOUT 32,000 years ago a land-bridge joined the Asian and North American continents at what is now the Bering Strait between Alaska and Siberia. Archaeologists believe that humans probably reached the North American continent by crossing this land-bridge.

The First Explorers

WHO WERE THE FIRST explorers? Probably early human beings who lived in Africa. According to evidence from fossils, ape-like creatures lived there about five million years ago. These creatures walked on two legs, had larger brains than apes, and used tools. From this evidence, scientists believe they were the ancestors of human beings. So far, Africa is the only part of the world where such fossils have been found. Fossils indicate that the climate then was warm and sunny, so plants would grow well, providing plenty of fruit, as well as food for the animals.

INDONESIA

MOST SCIENTISTS believe that people reached Australia about 40,000 years ago, crossing a land-bridge that linked it to Asia. However, another theory suggests that people arrived by sea, from the islands of what is now Indonesia and New Guinea.

AUSTRALIA

5

THE EGYPTIANS EXPLORE

Akkadian merchants show their king the goods they have brought back.

WITHOUT THE RIVER NILE there would have been no ancient Egyptian civilisation. Why? Most of Egypt was dry and arid. But every year, the Nile flooded its banks, leaving layers of rich silt which made the land very fertile. Crops grew so well that the ancient Egyptians had plenty to eat, and enough to trade with neighbouring people. The Nile was also the best means of transporting goods, as the desert was too hot for people and too rough for most wheeled vehicles. So the river gave the ancient Egyptians produce to sell, and a way to transport it. This allowed Egypt's rulers to build up a powerful state.

Ivory

Baboons

Animal skins

Incense

MADE FROM myrrh and other plant gums, incense was used in religious ceremonies and for embalming dead bodies to make mummies.

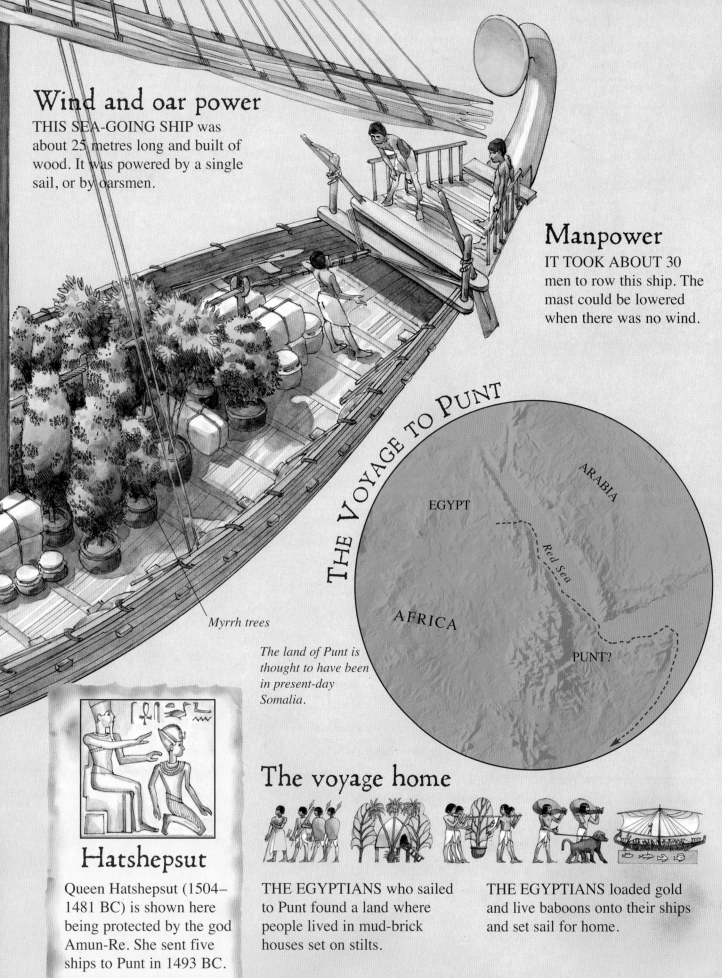

Wind and oar power

THIS SEA-GOING SHIP was about 25 metres long and built of wood. It was powered by a single sail, or by oarsmen.

Manpower

IT TOOK ABOUT 30 men to row this ship. The mast could be lowered when there was no wind.

Myrrh trees

THE VOYAGE TO PUNT

EGYPT

ARABIA

Red Sea

AFRICA

PUNT?

The land of Punt is thought to have been in present-day Somalia.

Hatshepsut

Queen Hatshepsut (1504–1481 BC) is shown here being protected by the god Amun-Re. She sent five ships to Punt in 1493 BC.

The voyage home

THE EGYPTIANS who sailed to Punt found a land where people lived in mud-brick houses set on stilts.

THE EGYPTIANS loaded gold and live baboons onto their ships and set sail for home.

THE GREEK EMPIRE

Alexander the Great

JRADE LEADS TO EXPLORATION – or is it the other way round? Certainly the peoples of the eastern Mediterranean were great sailors and traders. To buy tin, the Phoenicians (from present-day Lebanon) probably reached Cornwall, England around 500 BC. Early Greeks went to the Black Sea to find gold. Later, in the 5th century BC, Hanno the Greek traded along the west coast of Africa. He brought back tales of 'hairy women' – probably chimpanzees!

Alexander the Great led his army over huge distances, conquering Persia (present-day Iran) and travelling through Central Asia to India. He died in 323 BC, aged 32, but is still famous for his skill as a military leader.

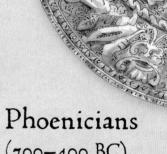

Phoenicians
(700–400 BC)

PHOENICIAN traders sailed all round the Mediterranean, and beyond. Powered by oarsmen and a single sail, their ships could carry a lot of cargo. The Phoenicians were also famous for luxury goods, such as silverware (above).

Alexander the Great

> I could be Alexander the Wonderful or Alexander the Traveller!

EUROPE

1

2

Mediterranean Sea

4

AFRICA

Alexander's travels

1   *334 BC – Alexander sets out from Greece to conquer Asia.*

2   *Defeats strong Persian army at Granicus river.*

3   *332 BC – Marches south; captures rich ports of Tyre and Sidon.*

4   *Goes to Egypt; founds city of Alexandria.*

5   *New war with Persians; goes back to Mesopotamia (present-day Iraq); defeats Persian king Darius at Gaugamela, 331 BC.*

6   *Heads east across wild country chasing Darius.*

7   *330 BC – Darius dies; Alexander marches north; crosses the Khyber Pass, almost 4000 metres above sea level.*

8   *328–327 BC – Captures remote kingdom of Bactria; leads army through mountains towards India.*

9   *326 BC – Crosses Indus river. Wants to explore India, but army mutinies.*

10   *Travels west along Indus; proves it is not connected to the Nile.*

11   *Divides his army; some men sail home, others travel by land.*

12   *Marches by night (when cooler) 321 kilometres through hot, barren desert; many men die.*

13   *Fleet short of food and water; mutiny feared. Overland marchers meet fleet at Hormuz; all head inland.*

14   *323 BC Alexander dies, aged 32, at Babylon.*

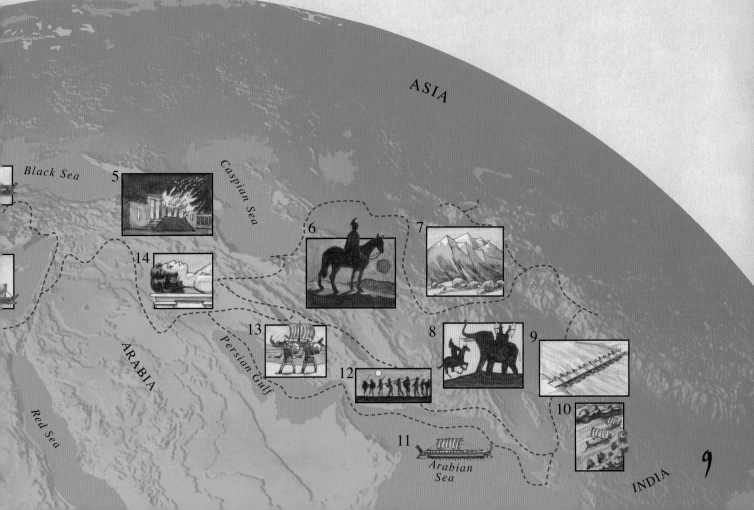

ROME: THE EMPIRE GROWS

Roman merchant ship

AROUND 900 BC, centuries before Alexander the Great was born, the city of Rome began. It would grow to be the capital of an empire which was larger and longer-lasting than Alexander's. The well-trained Roman army achieved this by conquest, and by good adminstration of the conquered lands, which allowed trade to flourish. Although the conquered states hated being under Roman control, their merchants welcomed the chance to trade with other parts of the empire. The Roman navy was as powerful as its army, and protected merchant ships from pirates.

Wise men

THE BIBLE tells how 'wise men' travelled from the East to Bethlehem to see the newborn Jesus.

Romans abroad!

These barbarians don't seem pleased to see us!

The Roman Empire

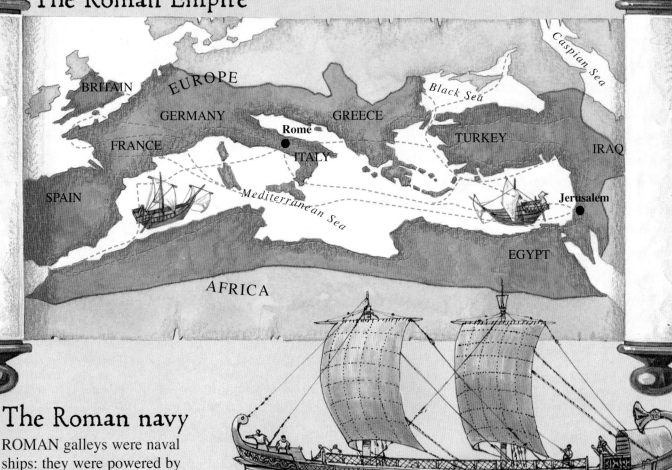

The Roman navy

ROMAN galleys were naval ships: they were powered by oarsmen (usually slaves) as well as sails. They were fast and easy to manoeuvre.

Roman galley

AS THE EMPIRE grew in power and wealth, Roman merchants quickly exploited the ready market for imported goods from China and Central Asia. This network of trade routes reached far beyond the Roman Empire.

Roman roads

paving stones
kerbstones
cement
concrete
sand
ditch
groma (a surveying instrument)

THE ROMANS built good roads throughout their empire so their soldiers could march as quickly as possible. However, merchants soon realised that good roads and direct routes also made transporting goods easier.

Tourism

IN GREECE, Romans visited Athens and, for their health, the temple of Asclepius at Epidaurus.

CROSSING OCEANS

This elegant dish was shipped from China to Iran around AD 800.

CHINESE MERCHANTS BEGAN TRADING with cities along the shores of the Indian Ocean about AD 479. They sold porcelain, silk and tea, and bought ivory, gold and spices. In 1403 Emperor Yong Le despatched about 300 ships laden with treasure under Admiral Zheng He. This was a voyage of exploration, and the emperor wished to form alliances with other rulers.

THE VOYAGES OF ZHENG HE

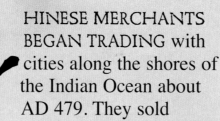

I speak Chinese and Arabic

What languages do you speak, Admiral?

Chinese sailing ships

THIS 15TH-CENTURY Chinese map suggests that Chinese sailing ships had sailed round the southern tip of Africa and reached the Atlantic Ocean.

Cape of Good Hope

Between 1403 and 1424 Zheng He's fleet made seven voyages, visiting many different lands.

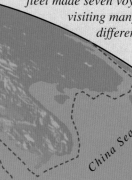

INDIA

CHINA

Bay of Bengal

ARABIA

China Sea

INDIAN OCEAN

Chinese sailing vessel

Maori people

AROUND AD 1000, the Maori people reached New Zealand. Centuries earlier their ancestors had left the islands now called Hawaii. Travelling in big ocean-going canoes, they settled the Pacific islands.

BY the 15th century, the biggest Chinese ships were far larger than any European ones. They had crews of 200 men and could carry nearly 1000 passengers, as well as 1000 tonnes of cargo. Columbus crossed the Atlantic with three ships about 20 metres long, and he had a total of 120 men.

Pacific islanders

SCATTERED across the Pacific Ocean are thousands of small islands whose inhabitants reached them centuries ago. Some time between AD 1000 and 1600, the people of Rapa Nui (Easter Island) carved stone figures 12 metres high, probably to guard their dead.

VIKINGS: RAIDERS TO TRADERS

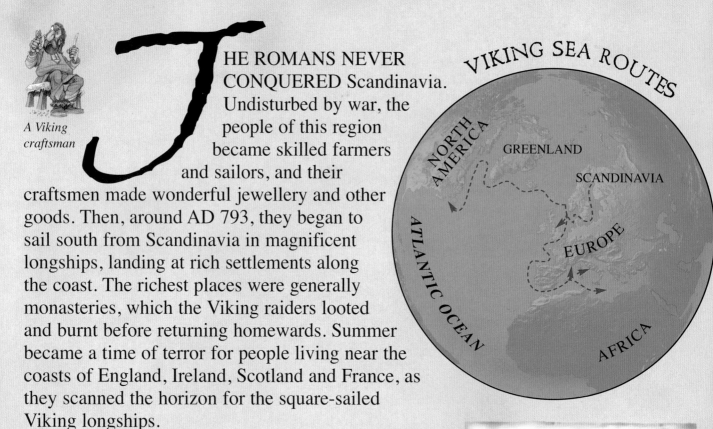

A Viking craftsman

THE ROMANS NEVER CONQUERED Scandinavia. Undisturbed by war, the people of this region became skilled farmers and sailors, and their craftsmen made wonderful jewellery and other goods. Then, around AD 793, they began to sail south from Scandinavia in magnificent longships, landing at rich settlements along the coast. The richest places were generally monasteries, which the Viking raiders looted and burnt before returning homewards. Summer became a time of terror for people living near the coasts of England, Ireland, Scotland and France, as they scanned the horizon for the square-sailed Viking longships.

VIKING SEA ROUTES

NORTH AMERICA
GREENLAND
SCANDINAVIA
ATLANTIC OCEAN
EUROPE
AFRICA

Viking sea routes

- ->

Vikings cross the Atlantic

IN EUROPE Viking raiders met little opposition, but it was different in Vinland (present-day Canada). When Leif Eriksson reached there around AD 1000, all was peaceful. But in AD 1002 Leif's brother Thorwald was killed when he attacked a group of Native Americans.

So much for `Vinland' (Wine land) being the land of wine!

This turf hut will see us through the winter.

Viking merchants

Slaves

SWEDISH Vikings were traders rather than raiders, selling amber, timber, fish and furs and buying wine, spices and silk from the Middle East and southern Europe.

Viking ships overland

Vikings travelling east through Russia, sailing mostly on rivers. Between rivers, they dragged their boats overland.

Viking longship

Knorr

Viking ships

VIKING longships were narrow and streamlined, and could be sailed or rowed. All Viking ships had a shallow draught, so could be run ashore easily. Knorrs or merchant ships were shorter and wider, and were used to carry large loads.

VIKING RAIDERS took everything from gold to people. But why return to the cold north when the climate was better further south? Gradually they began to stay, settle and marry. So, by around 1100, their descendants had become farmers and craftsmen.

Navigation

THE VIKINGS were skilful sailors. They used a device called a navigation table to help them find the way. The needle in the centre measured the height of the sun. The navigator could move a bar around the notched edge of the table to plot the ship's course.

15

MUSLIM EXPLORERS

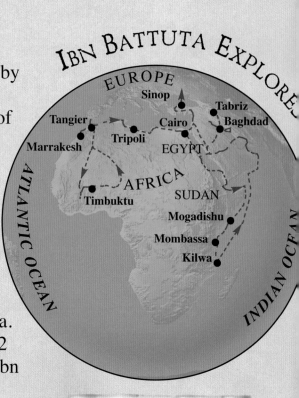

Medieval Muslim map of the world, with Mecca at the centre

T HE RELIGION OF ISLAM was founded by Muhammad in Arabia around AD 600. Many of his followers travelled widely to spread their faith. Islam encouraged scholarship and learning, and for many centuries Islamic scholars were far more advanced than those in Europe, especially in maths, science and medicine. Many of the ancient Greeks' discoveries survive only because early Islamic scholars recorded them. One scholar, Ibn Fadlan, travelled extensively in northern Russia. His vivid description of a Viking funeral in AD 922 is unique, as the Vikings left few written records. Ibn Battuta (1304–1377) was the greatest Muslim traveller. Born in Tangier, North Africa, he travelled throughout Africa, India and China.

IBN BATTUTA EXPLORE

EUROPE
Sinop
Tangier · Tabriz
Cairo · Baghdad
Marrakesh · Tripoli
EGYPT
ATLANTIC OCEAN
AFRICA
Timbuktu · SUDAN
Mogadishu
Mombassa
Kilwa
INDIAN OCEAN

Route of Ibn Battuta
------------------>

Ibn Battuta

We have travelled over 120,000 kilometres.

There is so much to see in the world!

Al-Idrisi

BORN in North Africa around 1100, al-Idrisi was a great explorer and cartographer. Unfortunately, his greatest achievement, a map of the world engraved on a silver disk, has not survived.

Ibn Fadlan meets the Vikings

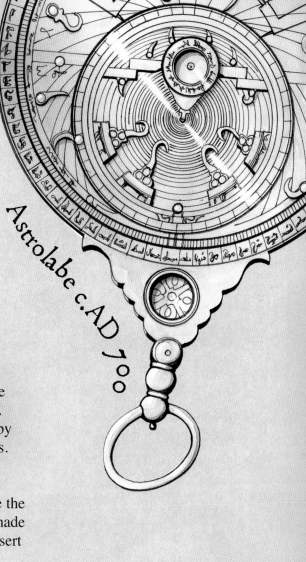

IBN FADLAN tells how a dead Viking chief was put in his longship, together with his weapons, dead horses and dogs. His favourite slave-girl was given a drink which seemed to drug her, and she was taken on board and killed. Finally the ship was set ablaze.

TRAVELLING by day in the heat of Arabia is impossible. Instead, explorers travelled by night, navigating by the stars. The astrolabe was invented around AD 700 by Muslim astronomers to help measure the positions of the stars. This made crossing the vast Arabian desert much easier.

Mecca

ALL MUSLIMS should make at least one pilgrimage (hajj) to the city of Mecca. There they visit the Kaaba, Islam's most sacred shrine.

THE OTTOMAN emperors of Turkey employed and encouraged scholars. They studied medicine, astronomy, science and maths, and their magnificent mosques show their technical skills.

Travels by camel

CAMELS provided transport in the desert lands which most Muslim travellers explored. They can go for a long time without eating or drinking.

MARCO POLO'S TRAVELS

UPON REACHING the Persian Gulf, the Polos continued inland, braving harsh desert winds

ONE OF THE GREATEST European travellers of the Middle Ages was Marco Polo (1254–1324). He left his home city of Venice in 1271, returning in 1295. In those 24 years he had travelled to China and explored India, Malaysia and Central Asia. Or had he? Some historians doubt it. He brought back many stories about the exotic places he had seen, and the tales were written down by Rustichello of Pisa, an author of romantic stories. Were these tales exaggerated by either Marco, Rustichello, or even by both? Some of the things he described seem too fantastic to be true.

Fact or fiction?

Hmmm, I think the khan would like to see you...

Family travels

MARCO'S father and uncle visited China between 1260 and 1269. In 1271 they went again, this time taking Marco too.

Meeting the Pope

AT ACRE (in present-day Israel) the Polos met Pope Gregory. He gave them a letter to give to Kublai Khan, ruler of the Mongols of central Asia.

Hot and cold

TRAVELLING conditions were difficult for the Polos. Days were hot, nights cold, and the ground stony and rough. As they went further east there were also mountain ranges to cross.

Kublai Khan

IN 1275 the party reached Kublai Khan's summer palace at Shengdu. The khan questioned the Polos about their travels and he made Marco a roving ambassador – and a spy. Or so Marco later claimed.

Prisoners

KUBLAI KHAN kept the Polos as virtual prisoners for nearly 20 years. He finally agreed they could go – if they escorted Princess Kokachin to her wedding in the Middle East.

MARCO POLO'S TRAVELS

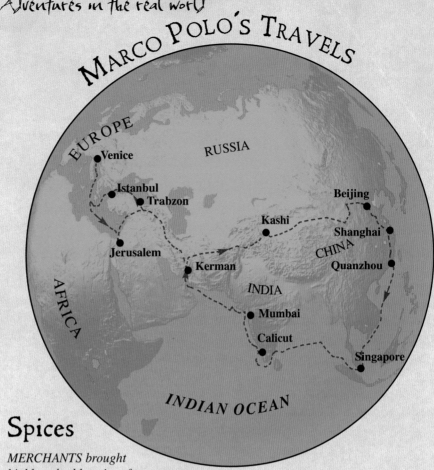

EUROPE · RUSSIA · Venice · Istanbul · Trabzon · Beijing · Kashi · Shanghai · Jerusalem · Kerman · CHINA · Quanzhou · AFRICA · INDIA · Mumbai · Calicut · Singapore · INDIAN OCEAN

Spices

MERCHANTS brought highly valuable spices from the east to Europe.

Cinnamon

Nutmeg

Cloves

Pepper

Reported route of
Marco Polo
----------------------->

CHINESE JUNKS were used to import spices from India and south-east Asia to the Middle East and Europe.

Home at last

THE POLOS sailed from Trebizond (present-day Trabzon) on the Black Sea to Venice.

Dog-headed cannibals?

MANY spices came from the Andaman Islands in the Indian Ocean – along with travellers' tales about dog-headed cannibals!

A prisoner again

IN 1298, during a war between Venice and Genoa, Marco Polo was imprisoned by the Genoese. They accused him of lying about his travels.

1492 – AMERICA!

Columbus' coat of arms

IN AUGUST 1492, three ships sailed from Spain commanded by Christopher Columbus. They were heading west, out into the Atlantic Ocean, far beyond the islands of the Azores (discovered in 1418). For centuries, many people had believed the world was flat. (The ancient Greeks knew it wasn't, but that knowledge had been lost.) If the world was flat, going too far from land would mean falling over the edge. But educated people like King Ferdinand and Queen Isabella of Spain knew better. They funded Columbus' voyage, hoping to find new sources of valuable spices in the East Indies.

Paying for the expedition

If necessary I will sell my jewels to pay for this expedition.

ISABELLA and Ferdinand ruled Spain together. They gave Columbus the money for his voyage.

The 'New' World

IN OCTOBER 1492 Columbus landed on the Bahamas. He reached South America on his third voyage and Central America on his fourth.

It's THAT way, I keep telling you!

The world in 1490

THIS MAP, drawn in 1490 by the German scholar Henricus Martellus, shows the countries known to European scholars and sailors. There is, of course, no sign of America.

THE VOYAGES OF CHRISTOPHER COLUMBUS

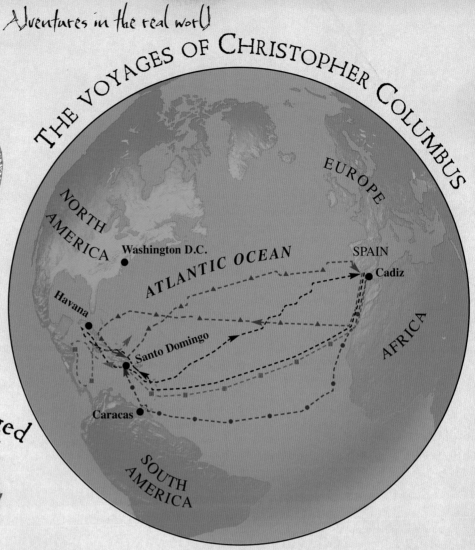

Lateen to square-rigged

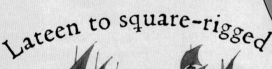

COLUMBUS' SHIPS were the *Santa Maria*, the *Pinta* and the *Niña*. He changed their triangular lateen sails, as used in the Mediterranean, to stronger square sails.

Voyage One ----▲----▲---→
Voyage Two ----------------→
Voyage Three --●----●----●--→
Voyage Four --■----■----■--→

BETWEEN 1492 and 1504 Columbus made four voyages to the so-called 'New World'. He didn't know he had discovered a continent – he thought he had found a new route to Asia.

The magnetic compass

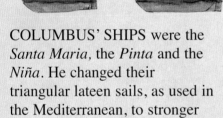

THE MAGNETIC compass was developed by the Chinese between 55 BC and AD 1064 . Arabian scholars had access to it by 1220. The European boxed compass, developed around 1190, made long-distance navigation much easier.

Amerigo Vespucci

ITALIAN NAVIGATOR Amerigo Vespucci moved to Spain when he was 39. He helped to equip the ships for Christopher Columbus' third expedition. He then set sail to South America himself, writing an account of his travels. It was his name that was given to South America, then later to the whole American continent.

I found the way to America? Bah! It was Asia, I tell you!

AROUND THE WORLD

Magellan and his crew witnessed the violent storms of the South American coast

EVEN THOUGH COLUMBUS BELIEVED he had reached Asia, others realised he hadn't. The Portuguese soldier Ferdinand Magellan (1480–1521) was one of them. By 1517 he was sure it was possible to sail around the world by heading west, on a more southerly route than Columbus had taken. In 1519 he set out with a fleet of five ships, paid for by the Spanish king. The voyage was plagued by sabotage, mutinies and storms. The final disaster was Magellan's death in 1521 on the island of Cebu. Eventually, in September 1522, the *Victoria*, the only remaining ship, returned to Spain. Only about 30 of the original 237 men had survived – the first people to sail around the world and prove Magellan was right.

No plain sailing!

If we go that way, we can be the first round the world.

The Magellan Strait

IT WAS BELIEVED that there was no way to get round the 'new' continent lying between Europe and the East Indies. But in October 1520 Magellan discovered a channel linking the Atlantic and Pacific oceans – now called the Magellan Strait.

The Spice Islands

THE RULER of Ternate, one of the Spice Islands, sent his royal barge – a huge outrigger canoe – to look at the *Trinidad* and *Victoria*, the two surviving ships from Magellan's expedition.

The Philippines

THE PHILIPPINES were named in honour of Prince Philip, the king of Spain's son. Without the king's financial help the voyage would have been impossible.

THE VOYAGES OF MAGELLAN

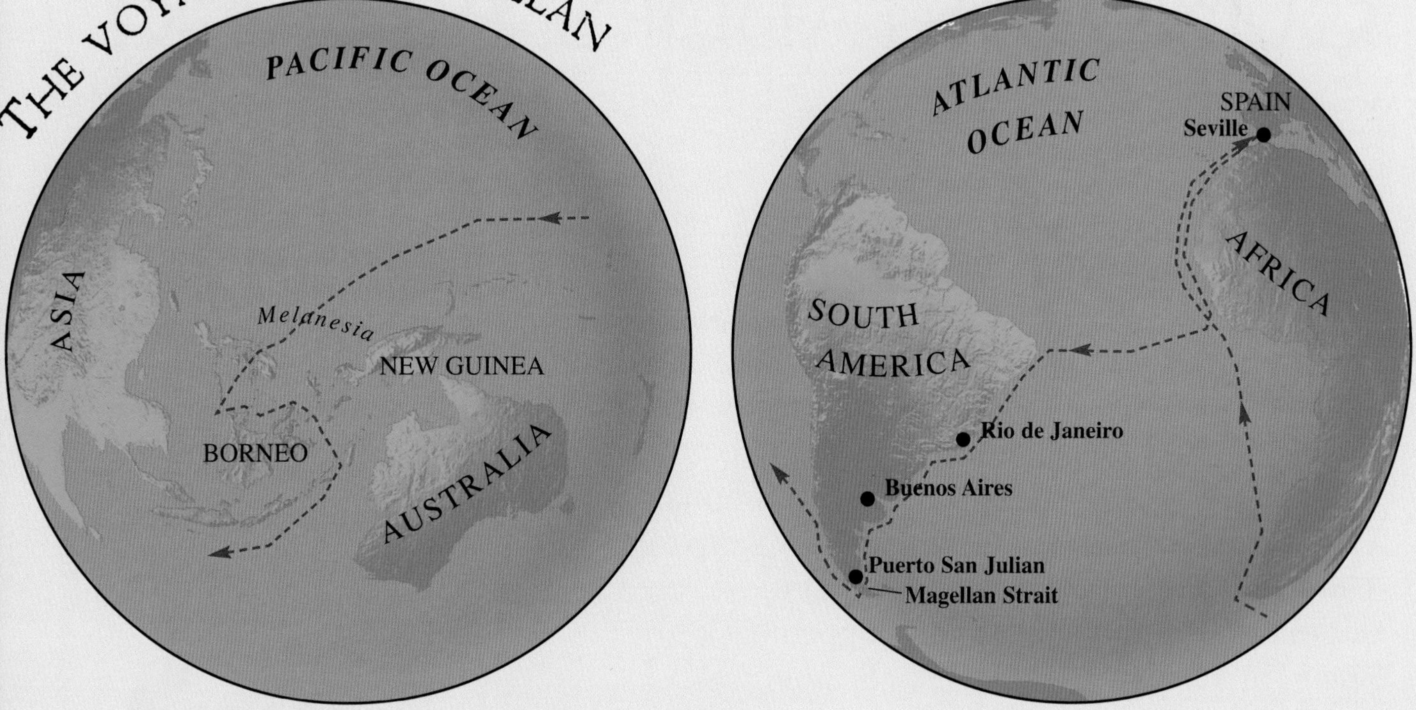

PACIFIC OCEAN

ASIA

Melanesia

NEW GUINEA

BORNEO

AUSTRALIA

ATLANTIC OCEAN

SPAIN
Seville

SOUTH AMERICA

AFRICA

Rio de Janeiro

Buenos Aires

Puerto San Julian
— Magellan Strait

THE EXPLOITS of Magellan and his surviving crew were even greater than those of Columbus. They went further, even though their ships were of poor quality, and they faced Portuguese attacks in the East Indies and in European waters.

The route taken by Magellan and, after his death, by Juan Sebastián del Cano on their epic voyage.

-------------------------------->

Magellan is killed

THE PEOPLE OF CEBU treated Magellan and his exhausted sailors so well that he agreed to help them in a battle with Mactan islanders. Unfortunately, Magellan was killed in the fighting.

My armour won't save me!

23

CONQUISTADORS ATTACK!

One of de Soto's ships

AFTER COLUMBUS' 1492 VOYAGE, other Europeans sailed westward. Columbus found little gold, but he returned with stories of people living in golden cities. The Spanish king sent the *conquistador* (Spanish for 'conqueror') Hernán Cortés to Mexico to see if these stories were true. The Aztec cities were not golden, but they were full of gold treasures that could be shipped back to Spain. In Peru, the rich Inca civilisation was plundered for Spain by Francisco Pizarro. The Spaniards claimed they were bringing Christianity to these people, but this was a flimsy excuse to take their wealth and destroy their civilisations. Within a few years of Cortés landing in Mexico, 90 per cent of the Aztecs were killed.

Spain takes control

Gulp!

Stop breathing down my neck – aaargh!

Outgunned

AZTEC WARRIORS believed that Cortés and his followers represented an ancient Aztec priest-king, Quetzalcoatl. When they discovered the truth, it was too late. Their weapons were useless against the firepower of Spanish guns.

Moctezuma

MOCTEZUMA, the ruler of the Aztecs, met with Cortés in 1519.

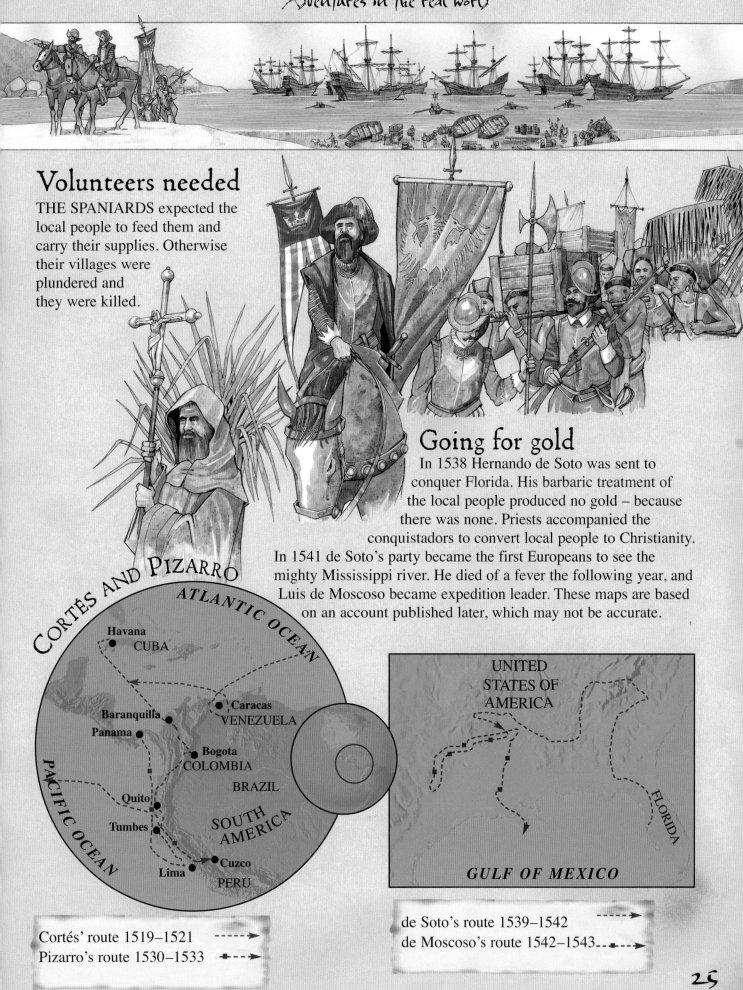

Volunteers needed

THE SPANIARDS expected the local people to feed them and carry their supplies. Otherwise their villages were plundered and they were killed.

Going for gold

In 1538 Hernando de Soto was sent to conquer Florida. His barbaric treatment of the local people produced no gold – because there was none. Priests accompanied the conquistadors to convert local people to Christianity. In 1541 de Soto's party became the first Europeans to see the mighty Mississippi river. He died of a fever the following year, and Luis de Moscoso became expedition leader. These maps are based on an account published later, which may not be accurate.

CORTÉS AND PIZARRO

ATLANTIC OCEAN

Havana
CUBA

Caracas
VENEZUELA

Baranquilla
Panama

Bogota
COLOMBIA

BRAZIL

PACIFIC OCEAN

Quito

Tumbes

SOUTH
AMERICA

Cuzco
Lima
PERU

UNITED
STATES OF
AMERICA

FLORIDA

GULF OF MEXICO

Cortés' route 1519–1521 - - - - ►
Pizarro's route 1530–1533 ◼- - - ►

de Soto's route 1539–1542 - - - - ►
de Moscoso's route 1542–1543 ◼- - -

25

DRAKE AND RALEIGH

Poop —

Officers' cabins

Tobacco reached Europe from America in the 16th century

ENVIOUS OF SPANISH DOMINANCE in the New World, Queen Elizabeth I of England was keen to find a North-West Passage to the Spice Islands. The country that found this route would become very powerful. Francis Drake – the first Englishman to see the Pacific Ocean – was chosen to command this secret expedition, and on 15 November 1577 he sailed from Plymouth on a journey that would take him around the world. Drake's navigational skills were extraordinary. When he returned, the queen found that her investment of £1,000 in the expedition had brought her £47,000 in return. Drake was allowed to keep £10,000, and was knighted on board his ship, the *Golden Hind*.

Rudder

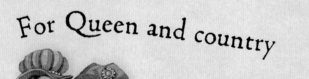

For Queen and country

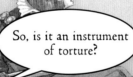

So, is it an instrument of torture?

It's a prickly pear, Ma'am – I believe you can eat it.

SIR WALTER RALEIGH (1552–1618) was another English explorer. He organised expeditions to North America, bringing back potatoes, tomatoes and prickly pears. He went to South America to find El Dorado (the city of gold), but failed because it is a mythical place and doesn't exist.

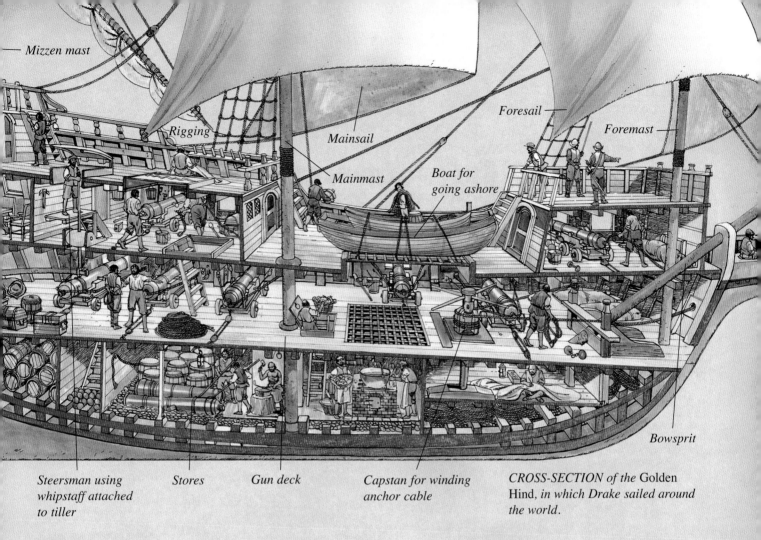

Mizzen mast

Rigging

Mainsail

Mainmast

Boat for going ashore

Foresail

Foremast

Bowsprit

Steersman using whipstaff attached to tiller

Stores

Gun deck

Capstan for winding anchor cable

CROSS-SECTION of the Golden Hind, *in which Drake sailed around the world.*

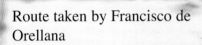

Route taken by Francisco de Orellana

- - - - - - - - - - - - - - - - →

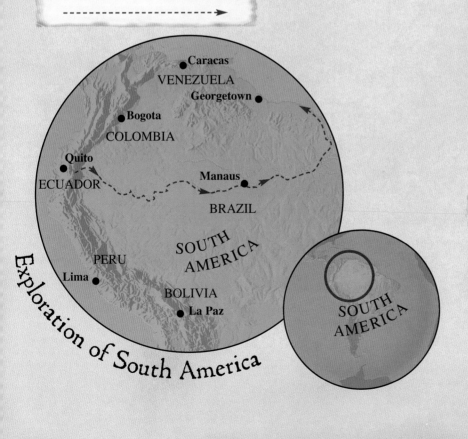

Caracas

VENEZUELA

Georgetown

Bogota

COLOMBIA

Quito

ECUADOR

Manaus

BRAZIL

SOUTH AMERICA

PERU

Lima

BOLIVIA

La Paz

SOUTH AMERICA

Exploration of South America

South America

SOUTH AMERICA was a magnet for 16th-century explorers seeking gold. In 1542 Francisco de Orellana became the first European to sail up the River Amazon. He returned with tales of warrior women – the fabled Amazons. Walter Raleigh searched for gold further north, but found neither gold nor Amazons.

GALLEON 1586

Sandglasses were used to tell the time at sea

T HE GALLEONS OF the late 16th century were steered with a whipstaff – a long lever connected by a hinge (called the gooseneck) to the tiller. The tiller moved the rudder from side to side. The whipstaff was operated by a helmsman, who stood below decks and could not see out.

Sailors

CAPTAINS wanted men with as much sea experience as possible. Sailors were rarely keen to join dangerous voyages, so captains often lied about their destination. By the time the truth was discovered, it would be too late for the sailors to change their minds!

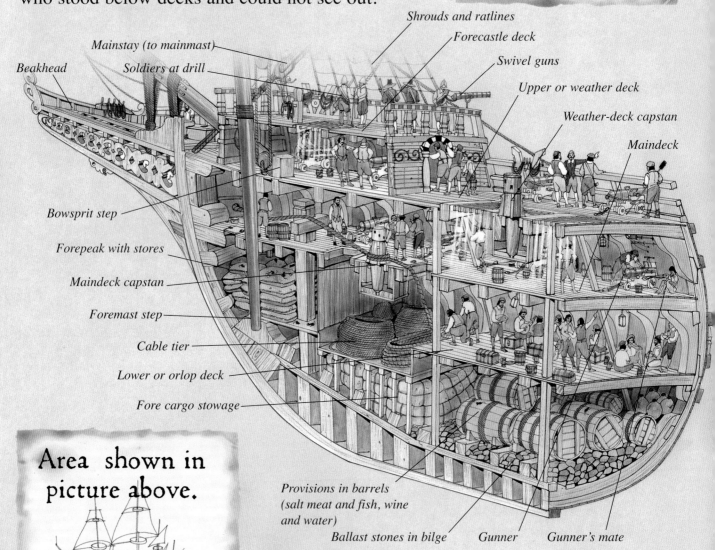

- Shrouds and ratlines
- Forecastle deck
- Mainstay (to mainmast)
- Swivel guns
- Beakhead
- Soldiers at drill
- Upper or weather deck
- Weather-deck capstan
- Maindeck
- Bowsprit step
- Forepeak with stores
- Maindeck capstan
- Foremast step
- Cable tier
- Lower or orlop deck
- Fore cargo stowage
- Provisions in barrels (salt meat and fish, wine and water)
- Ballast stones in bilge
- Gunner
- Gunner's mate

Area shown in picture above.

Life on board

The smell below decks was terrible – not just from unwashed bodies and clothes, but also from all the ship's waste, which ended up in the bilge with the ballast stones.

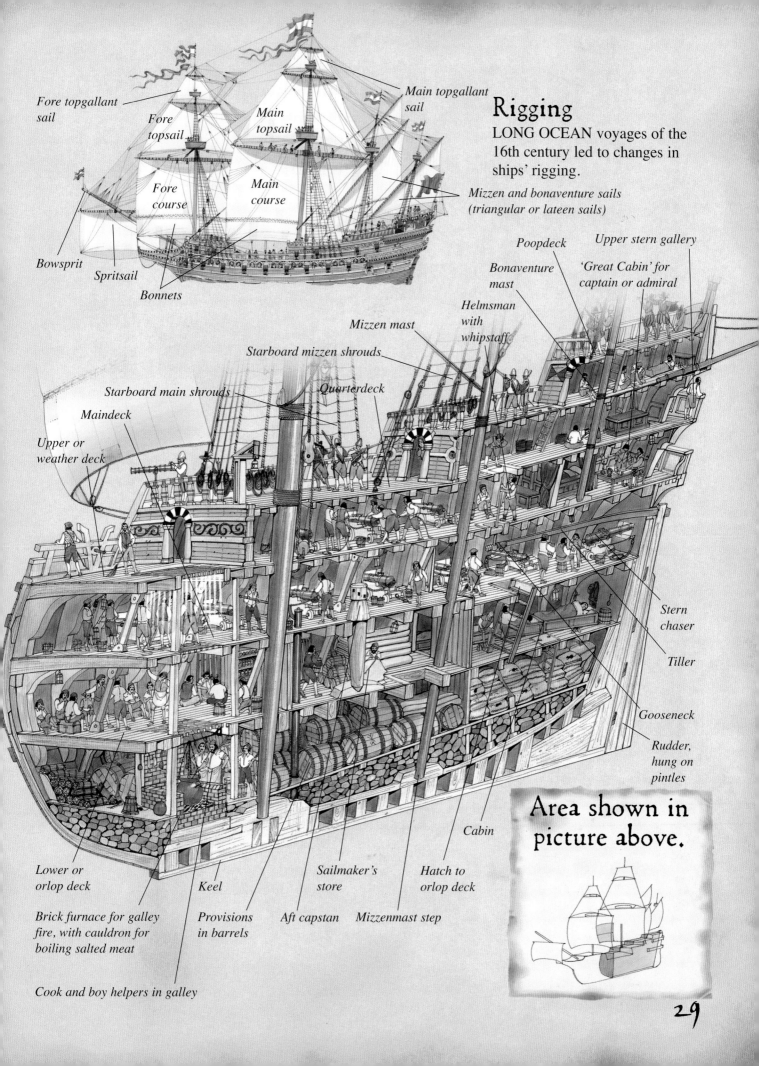

Fore topgallant sail

Fore topsail

Main topsail

Main topgallant sail

Fore course

Main course

Rigging
LONG OCEAN voyages of the 16th century led to changes in ships' rigging.

Mizzen and bonaventure sails (triangular or lateen sails)

Bowsprit

Spritsail

Bonnets

Poopdeck

Bonaventure mast

Upper stern gallery

'Great Cabin' for captain or admiral

Helmsman with whipstaff

Mizzen mast

Starboard mizzen shrouds

Quarterdeck

Starboard main shrouds

Maindeck

Upper or weather deck

Stern chaser

Tiller

Gooseneck

Rudder, hung on pintles

Cabin

Lower or orlop deck

Keel

Sailmaker's store

Hatch to orlop deck

Brick furnace for galley fire, with cauldron for boiling salted meat

Provisions in barrels

Aft capstan

Mizzenmast step

Cook and boy helpers in galley

Area shown in picture above.

29

A New Life

Seal of the first English company to trade in North America, the Virginia Company

AS MORE SHIPS SAILED to and from the New World, navigators and sailors became more experienced – but it was still a dangerous journey. The voyage lasted several months, and 13-metre-high waves could easily swamp the small wooden ships. But many people were prepared to face such danger – some seeking adventure, some riches, and others prompted by religion. Early in the 16th century King Henry VIII of England broke with the Roman Catholic Church and established the Protestant Church of England. The country changed between Catholic and Protestant under several successive rulers. Persecution was common, and some felt it was safer to risk the dangers of the journey to the New World than to remain in England.

The Algonquins

NATIVE AMERICANS of the Algonquin nation were among the first to have their lands taken from them by European settlers.

Stockades

SSSSSHH! Did you hear that?!

Maybe England would have been safer after all.

THE ALGONQUINS lived in villages surrounded by stockades, and built homes of saplings, bark and matting.

SETTLERS BROUGHT European ways with them, including firearms and armour. But armour made it difficult to move through the dense surrounding forests.

The Mayflower

Cargo stored in barrels

Living quarters

Pilgrim Fathers

IN 1620 the *Mayflower* sailed from England with around 100 people on board: the 'Pilgrim Fathers'. They were going to start a new life free from religious persecution.

IT IS estimated that 35 million Americans – 12% of the total population – are direct descendants of those first *Mayflower* Pilgrims.

Thanksgiving Day

PILGRIM FAMILIES celebrated their first harvest in their new homeland on Thanksgiving Day, 1621. They did not celebrate later harvests – but in 1863 President Abraham Lincoln finally made Thanksgiving Day a permanent national holiday in America.

Attacks

ATTACKS WERE always a danger for villages like Wolstenholme Towne, built up-river from Jamestown, Virginia in 1620. This village prospered, but between 1606 and 1625 over 6,000 of the 7,000 people who sailed to a new life in Virginia had died.

Strong stockade

FRENCH EXPLORERS

Jean Nicolet

IT WAS NOT JUST BRITAIN, Portugal and Spain who explored and exploited the American continent – French explorers were also there. Etienne Brûlé probably explored the Great Lakes, but left no record of his travels. Others searched for the route to China and the riches that they thought they would find there. In 1634 Jean Nicolet set out to find the 'western sea', beyond which he believed he'd find China. No one then had any idea how huge the American continent is. Nicolet never found his western sea, but he explored the Great Lakes and was the first European to reach the Midwest.

Traders

IN CANADA Frenchmen called '*coureurs de bois*', (runners through the wood) travelled great distances to trade with the Indians.

THE WINNEBAGO INDIANS were amazed when they saw Nicolet dressed in a Chinese robe. Like many people, he thought North America was linked to China and it would be tactful to arrive wearing Chinese clothes. But he was actually on Lake Michigan's western shore!

Mistaken identity

La Salle names Louisiana and claims it for France.

Louisiana

THE WINNEBAGOES had told Nicolet of a great river flowing south: the Mississippi. In 1678 Robert Cavelier de la Salle set out from the Great Lakes to explore the river and reach its mouth. In April 1682 he reached the Gulf of Mexico. He claimed the land he had travelled through for France, and named it Louisiana after King Louis XIV.

SADLY, LOUIS XIV was not impressed. La Salle returned to the Mexican Gulf, where he was murdered in 1684.

THE NIAGARA FALLS, between Lakes Ontario and Erie, blocked la Salle's route. Though the French had heard about the Falls, the sight was still awesome. The expedition carried their boats around the Falls, then continued. In the group was a priest, Louis Hennepin. He spent years exploring in North America, and was captured by Sioux Indians. Later he wrote about his adventures – not always accurately.

Captain's log AD 1768-1779

COOK IN THE PACIFIC

Maori warriors

In the 18th century, Europeans knew very little about the South Pacific. The region was thought to contain a giant continent, stretching across the South Pole and reaching as far north as the Tropics. The Solomon Islands, New Zealand and possibly even Australia were all thought to be part of this huge landmass. Great Britain and France took the lead in exploring the South Pacific. It was the Englishman, Captain James Cook, whose three voyages to the South Seas between 1768 and 1779 finally resolved the mystery. His charts of the region, showing the Solomon Islands, New Zealand's North and South Islands, and the east coast of Australia, proved that they were all separate countries.

The Endeavour

Stores

The routes taken by Cook on his three voyages	1768–1771	------•------•------>
	1772–1775	------■------■------>
	1776–1779	------------------>

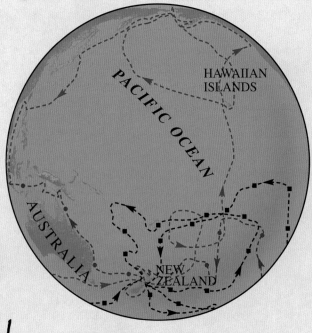

Wardroom

Barrels of fresh water

Living quarters

THE *ENDEAVOUR*, Cook's ship, had originally carried coal. It was strongly built and could carry 600 tonnes of cargo and crew – essential for the sort of expedition Cook was planning. He also needed space for the specimens he hoped to collect.

A globe which opens to show the positions of the stars and constellations.

A portable observatory

COOK took a portable observatory so he could study the stars, and became the first known person to see the transit of Venus.

EUROPEANS EXPLORE AFRICA

Many slaves were taken from Africa at this time

EUROPEANS HAVE BEEN TRADING with Africa for centuries, but until the 19th century, trade was only with coastal areas and lands north of the Sahara. The climate and geography made further exploration extremely difficult. In areas with high rainfall there was dense jungle, and in drier regions there was scrub. There were high mountains, deep valleys, and dangers ranging from big cats to tiny, disease-carrying insects. Waterfalls and rapids often made large rivers impassable, and many of the local people were understandably hostile to outsiders. But, as more of the Earth was explored, Africa and its unknown interior began to arouse interest.

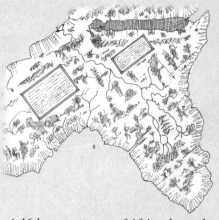

A 16th-century map of Africa drawn by Descalier, a French geographer. Based on sailors' reports, it is very accurate.

The River Niger

MUNGO PARK (1771–1806), a Scottish doctor, made the first scientific exploration of the River Niger in West Africa. He was drowned during an ambush.

Into Africa

Timbuktu

TALES OF TIMBUKTU tantalised European explorers. In 1826, Scotsman Alexander Laing (left) was first to reach the city. He was murdered soon afterwards. The Frenchman René-Auguste Caillié (right) was luckier – he got there in 1827 and survived.

CAMEL TRAINS transported goods such as salt, gold, cloth and slaves across the Sahara. They were also the only way for Europeans to cross the Sahara – but not without danger.

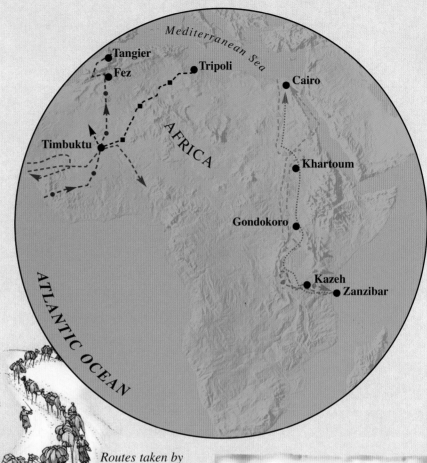

Routes taken by some European explorers of Africa in the 19th century.

Park	- - - - - - - - →
Caillié	- • - - • - - • - →
Laing	- ■ - - ■ - - ■ - →
Burton and Speke	- - - ◄ - - ◄ - →
Speke and Grant	· · · · · · · · →
The Bakers	◄ - - - - - - →

The source of the River Nile

SEVERAL EXPEDITIONS had tried, but failed, to find the Nile's source. In 1859 Englishman John Speke (left) thought he had found it, but fellow explorer Richard Burton (right) disagreed. Speke tried again, this time with James Grant. In July 1862 Speke was indeed proved correct.

AS THEY returned, Speke and Grant found the explorers Samuel and Barbara Baker waiting for them. The Bakers would become the first Europeans to see the Kabarega Falls in present-day Uganda.

The Bakers at the Kabarega Falls.

DOCTOR LIVINGSTONE?

Dr David Livingstone

JTWO OF THE BEST-KNOWN 19th-century explorers of Africa are David Livingstone (1813–1873), a Scottish doctor, and Henry Stanley (1841–1904), a Welsh journalist. In 1841 Livingstone went to southern Africa as a missionary. In 1848 he decided to explore the central part of Africa, and was the first European to see many of its magnificent sights, including the great waterfalls on the Zambezi River, which he named the Victoria Falls, after the British queen. By 1871 no-one had heard from him for three years. Sensing a good story, the editor of the *New York Herald* sent Henry Stanley, the paper's European correspondent, to find Dr Livingstone.

Mary Livingstone

MARY MOFFAT (1820–1862) married David Livingstone in 1845. The following years were difficult for her, with frequent moves and illnesses. She had six children, and sometimes suffered from partial paralysis. She and the children returned to England for four years in order for her to recover. After her death in 1862, Livingstone continued his missionary work for 11 more years.

The Zambezi River

You're not looking at lunch!

SUSA AND CHUMAH were Livingstone's servants but soon became his friends. They travelled with him on many of his expeditions.

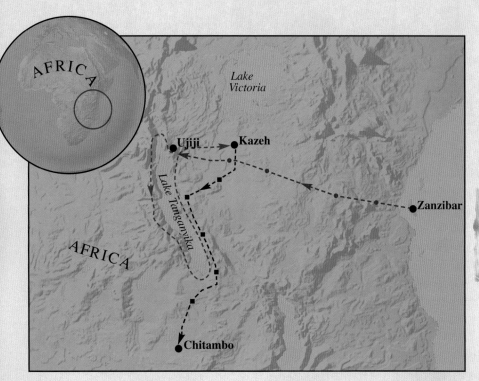

THE JOURNEYS made by Livingstone and Stanley, separately and together, between 1871 and 1873. Stanley's group took almost 14 months to travel the 3,500 kilometres from Zanzibar to Ujiji.

Stanley	---•---•---•---•---→
Livingstone	---■---■---■---→
Stanley and Livingstone	------→

'Dr Livingstone, I presume'

STANLEY FOUND Livingstone on 10 November 1871 in the trading town of Ujiji by Lake Tanganyika, and it made him famous. Livingstone's many years of exploring had damaged his health, and he was often too weak to walk. But he refused to return to England with Stanley, preferring to remain in Africa. Livingstone treated his African helpers well, and many were devoted to him. When he was found dead in May 1873, his servants buried his heart in Africa, then carried his body hundreds of miles to the coast in a journey that took nine months. Livingstone was given a state funeral in Westminster Abbey, London, on 18 April 1874.

Medical supplies

ILLNESS WAS one of the greatest threats facing Europeans in Africa. Every expedition had to take its own medical supplies. This is Stanley's medical chest.

Henry Morton Stanley

Dr David Livingstone

WOMEN EXPLORERS

Mary Kingsley

ON 19TH-CENTURY EUROPE women's lives were usually restricted to marrying and having children. They were not expected to be explorers. But some women did indeed explore Africa: Dutch Alexine Tinne explored the Nile south of Khartoum, American-born May French-Sheldon led an expedition to Mount Kilimanjaro, and Englishwoman Mary Kingsley explored west and equatorial Africa. Born in 1862, Kingsley lived quietly with her parents for 30 years, but when they died, she went to Africa. She made two expeditions, from June to December 1893 and again from December 1894 to November 1895. She made so many discoveries and won so much respect that she was appointed an adviser to the government. She died, aged only 38, working as a nurse in South Africa during the Boer War.

The Fang people

KINGSLEY LIVED with the Fang people, who built their villages near the Ogooué River, in present-day Gabon. She studied their culture and thought it should be protected from European ways. She gave this carving of a Fang girl (below) to the British Museum in London.

Kingsley's visiting card

I wonder who will find it . . .

40

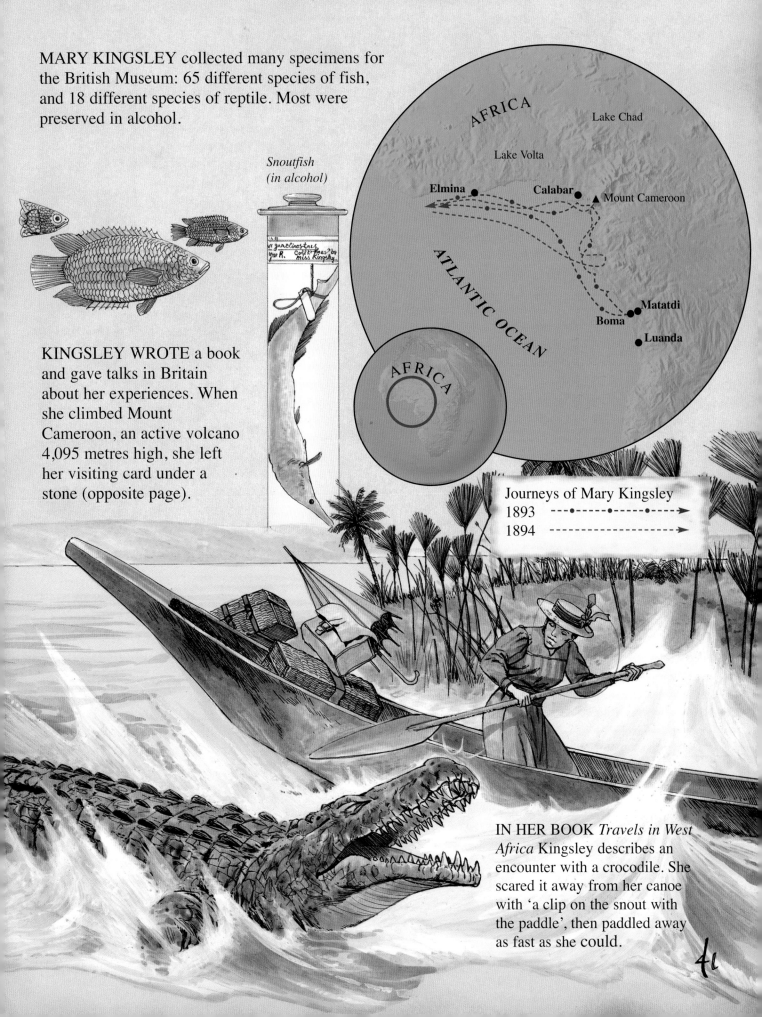

MARY KINGSLEY collected many specimens for the British Museum: 65 different species of fish, and 18 different species of reptile. Most were preserved in alcohol.

Snoutfish (in alcohol)

KINGSLEY WROTE a book and gave talks in Britain about her experiences. When she climbed Mount Cameroon, an active volcano 4,095 metres high, she left her visiting card under a stone (opposite page).

AFRICA

Lake Chad

Lake Volta

Elmina   Calabar   ▲ Mount Cameroon

ATLANTIC OCEAN

AFRICA

Matatdi
Boma
Luanda

Journeys of Mary Kingsley
1893 ------•------•------→
1894 ------------------→

IN HER BOOK *Travels in West Africa* Kingsley describes an encounter with a crocodile. She scared it away from her canoe with 'a clip on the snout with the paddle', then paddled away as fast as she could.

41

FROM COAST TO COAST

Indian basket and rattle

IN **1763**, after a successful military expedition, Britain took over France's lands in Canada. Slowly the British explored further west. News came that Captain Cook had been to Canada's west coast and found there was a market in China for Canadian furs. East-coast companies wanted a share of the trade, but needed an overland route. In 1789 Alexander Mackenzie was sent to find one, but the river he found (now named the Mackenzie) flowed into the Arctic Ocean. In 1792, after another very difficult journey, he finally succeeded. It took five weeks to reach the source of the Peace River in the Rockies. One river (now the Fraser) was too dangerous for canoes, so Mackenzie and his party went on foot – through snow, forests and over mountains – before finding a river that flowed to the Pacific.

The Pacific

IN 1808 Simon Fraser explored the river that Mackenzie had found too dangerous for canoes. The only way to get around some steep cliffs was on Native American ladders made of roots and bark, which swayed alarmingly in the wind.

> I've done it – I've reached the Pacific!

Carved in stone

'ALEX MACKENZIE from Canada by land 22nd July 1793.' Mackenzie carved this inscription on a rock near the Pacific Ocean to mark his achievement. It is still there, now preserved in red concrete.

MACKENZIE'S PARTY lost most of their supplies when their canoes capsized.

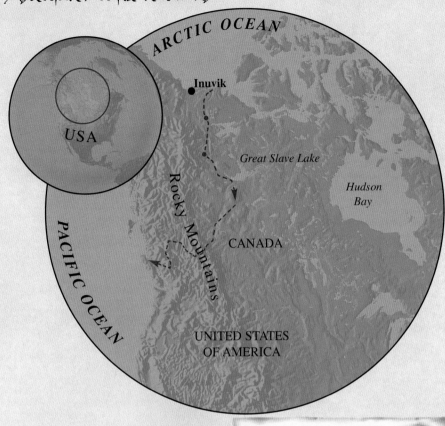

THE ROCKY MOUNTAINS had always stopped French and British fur traders crossing Canada. When Mackenzie reached the Pacific in July 1793, he became the first European to cross North America from coast to coast.

Journeys of Mackenzie
1789 ------●------●------●------→
1793 ----------------------------→

EUROPEAN EXPLORERS of North America relied heavily on Native Americans for local knowledge and to act as guides. Native Americans adapted their lives to their surroundings: those who lived in the dense forests were mostly hunters and trappers, while those on the plains were expert horsemen.

LEWIS AND CLARK

Fur traders

S INCE LA SALLE'S TIME (see page 33), Lousiana had remained largely unexplored. In 1803 the French emperor Napoleon sold the territory to America – the 'Louisiana Purchase'. US President Thomas Jefferson wanted an easy trade route to the Pacific coast. He chose two army officers, Meriwether Lewis and William Clark, to lead an expedition. They set off up the Missouri River in 1804, spending a bitter winter near a Mandan village in North Dakota. After many months of dangerous travel (horses fell over precipices and food was running out), the expedition reached the Pacific on 16 October 1805.

Trappers

THE FIRST European explorers of North America were fur trappers. Associations of merchants, like the Hudson's Bay Company of Canada, built well-defended trading posts such as Fort Garry. Many of these later grew into towns.

The call of the wild

On 13 June 1805 Lewis escaped from a grizzly bear by swimming a river.

You don't seem pleased to see me!

Lewis and Clark

Lewis (left) (1774–1809) and Clark (right) (1770–1838) made a good team. Lewis was a scholar, interested in scientific observation. Although a brilliant organiser, he was a quiet and rather distant man. Clark, however, was much more outgoing and an excellent second-in-command. Lewis later became Governor of Louisana.

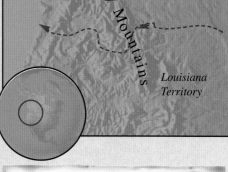

Journey of Lewis and Clark
across the Rocky Mountains

- ->

WHEN LEWIS AND CLARK left North Dakota they employed a Canadian *coureur de bois* (see page 32) who brought his Shoshone wife, Sacajawea.

Crossing the Rocky Mountains, they entered Shoshone lands. The chief was Sacajawea's brother. The Shoshones' help and advice allowed the expedition to

avoid some extremely dangerous rivers and reach the Pacific coast in safety.

A SPIRIT DANCE by Native Americans of the north-west coast. In their journals Lewis and Clark made valuable notes and observations on Native American life .

A CHINOOK CHIEF met the party by the mouth of the Columbia River, down which they travelled to the Pacific. Sacajawea did not speak his language, and so interpreted with signs.

45

THE WAY TO THE WEST

Settlers and gold prospectors followed dangerous cross-country trails

THE ROUTE FOUND by Lewis and Clark was far too difficult for regular travel. In February 1824 a party of trappers led by Jedediah Smith was travelling west when snow blocked their way. A Crow Indian told them of a more southerly route through the mountains. Smith and his party realised this was the ideal route to the west – they called it the South Pass.

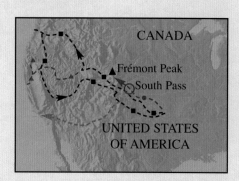

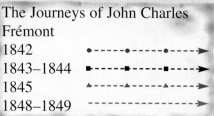

The Journeys of John Charles Frémont
1842
1843–1844
1845
1848–1849

TALES OF fortunes to be made in the west soon spread, and many people set out on the dangerous journey. But as yet there were no maps or marked routes. In 1842 the US government appointed army surveyor John Charles Frémont to map out the best routes.

Wrong mountain!

FRÉMONT'S nickname was 'the Great Pathfinder'. His books about his expeditions sold in huge numbers. He climbed the 'highest' peak in the Rockies, planting the American flag on the summit. It was a popular gesture, but he had chosen the wrong peak – there are higher ones!

California

IN 1845 Frémont's mapping work was interrupted by war between the US and Mexico. The unequal conflict didn't last long. Mexico lost California, which became the 31st state of America, and Frémont was appointed military governor. He became a millionaire after the gold rush of 1848, and was even nominated for the presidency in 1856.

Pyramid Lake

ALTHOUGH MUCH of Frémont's work was mapping sites that had already been discovered, he did make some new discoveries, including Pyramid Lake in Nevada.

ACROSS AUSTRALIA

Australia and Tasmania

CAPTAIN COOK HAD REPORTED good farming land in the area around Sydney. Unfortunately for the first settlers, he was wrong. Not until 1813 did British explorers find a way through the Great Dividing Range to the really fertile land beyond. Slowly, settlements grew up along the coast, but the searing heat of Australia's desert interior made it difficult to cross. Many explorers died in the attempt, including Robert Burke and William Wills. Camels were imported from Asia to carry explorers' equipment across the interior, as they are well adapted to high temperatures, little water and sandy terrain. They thrived, and there are still wild camels in Australia today.

Burke and Wills

ROBERT O'HARA Burke (left) (1820–1861) led the first known expedition to cross Australia from south to north. His party left in August 1860, but by February 1861 they could go no further and turned back. Burke, William Wills (right) (1834–1861) and John King returned to a deserted camp at Cooper's Creek. Exhausted and starving, Burke and Wills died in June 1861, but King survived and was rescued.

Surviving the desert

I need to change you for a camel!

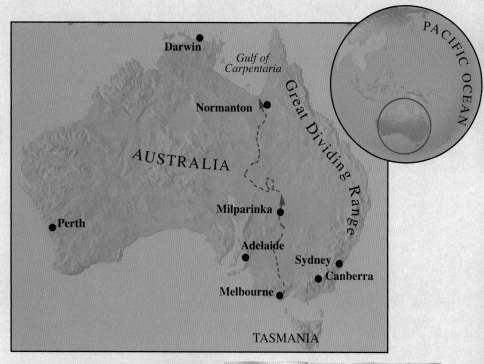

EUROPEAN explorers had problems with the climate, but Australia's native Aboriginal people had no such difficulties. Skilled trackers, they knew how and where to find food and water in the continent's dry wastes. Many expeditions employed them as guides.

Route of Burke and Wills's journey across Australia
------------------>

AUSTRALIA'S CLIMATE is harsh, so the Aboriginal people moved around to find food and water. But European settlers did not understand this, and drove them off the land the settlers were trying to farm, which caused conflict.

Adelaide

NAMED AFTER Queen Adelaide, consort of the British king William IV, the city was founded in 1836 as the capital of the province of South Australia. It was the starting point for many early expeditions into the Australian desert.

THE ABORIGINAL people have many sacred places in Australia's interior, where they hold special ceremonies.

TO THE NORTH POLE

Husky team

COLUMBUS' DISCOVERY OF AMERICA was exciting, but traders really wanted a westward route to Asia. So the search was on for a way around the 'new' continent. Magellan's southern route (see pages 22–23) was a long and difficult voyage. There was a northern route, but this was very dangerous, and was frozen for much of the year. Explorers also realised that there was an area around the North Pole that never thawed. So, in the 19th century, various governments started funding scientific expeditions to reach the North Pole.

Destination Asia?

IN 1576 Martin Frobisher, an English explorer searching for the North-West Passage, reached Baffin Island. The facial features of the Inuit people there made him think he had reached Asia.

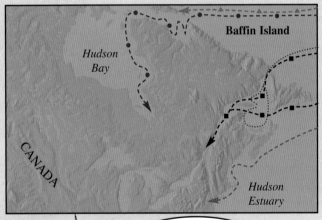

Baffin Island

Hudson Bay

CANADA

Hudson Estuary

Cartier 1534	....................➤	*Journeys by early explorers searching for a northerly route around America.*
Cartier 1535–1536	—■—■—■—➤	
Frobisher 1576	—▲—▲—▲—➤	
Hudson 1609	— — — — ➤	
Hudson 1610–1611	—●—●—●—➤	

Spears and bows are no match for our muskets.

FROBISHER and his men had a few skirmishes with the people of Baffin Island.

ARCTIC OCEAN

Bering Strait

North Pole

Kara Sea

GREENLAND

Barents Sea

Trapped in the Arctic

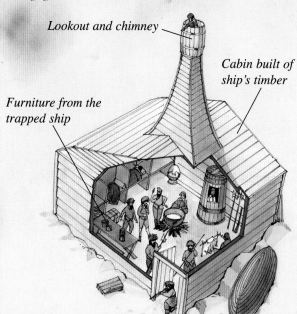

Lookout and chimney

Cabin built of ship's timber

Furniture from the trapped ship

Barents's journey 1596	●- - -●- - -●- - -▶
Amundsen's route 1903–1906	- - - - - - - - -▶
Peary's expedition 1909	◆- - -◼- - -◼- - -▶

TRADE HAD LED TO the search for the North-West Passage in the 16th century, but national pride was behind the race to the North Pole.

Willem Barents (died 1597)

IN 1596 DUTCHMAN Willem Barents's ship was trapped by the Arctic ice. His party built a cabin and survived the winter, but he died on the voyage home.

ROBERT PEARY (1856–1920), an American naval officer, was first to reach the North Pole in 1909 – it was his eighth attempt.

CHARLES HILL (1821–1871), another American, made three unsuccessful attempts to reach the North Pole. He died on the third.

NJ

NORGE

NORWEGIAN EXPLORER Roald Amundsen took an easier way to the North Pole in 1928 – by airship!

RACING SOUTHWARD

Shackleton's ship, the Endurance

ONCE THE NORTH POLE had been reached, the new challenge was the South Pole. Captain Robert Falcon Scott (1869–1912) had led the first British investigations of Antarctica in 1901–1914. On his second expedition, between 1910 and 1912, he intended to go to the South Pole. However, the Norwegian explorer Roald Amundsen, using Inuit methods learned in the Arctic, got there first. Amundsen's team chose a route along the narrow Axel Heiberg Glacier and headed for the Pole with plenty of supplies. Scott's journey was plagued by bad weather and his men died of cold and exhaustion on their way back to base camp.

Endurance

CRASSH!

Abandon ship!

Captain Robert Falcon Scott

SCOTT STARTED his ascent of Antarctica's Beardmore Glacier on 10 December 1911. His team arrived at the South Pole on 18 January 1912, only to find that Amundsen had beaten them. The weather on the return journey was savage, and blizzards made travel impossible. Scott was the last of the party to die, only 17 kilometres from his destination, on 29 March 1912.

Endurance against all the odds!

IN 1914 British explorer Ernest Shackleton (1874–1922) tried to cross Antarctica via the South Pole. After his ship, *Endurance*, was crushed in the ice, the crew had to take to the lifeboats. They travelled over 1,400 kilometres through icy storms to reach land. Shackleton and two crewmen travelled the last 240 kilometres alone to raise a rescue party for their stranded shipmates. The whole crew survived.

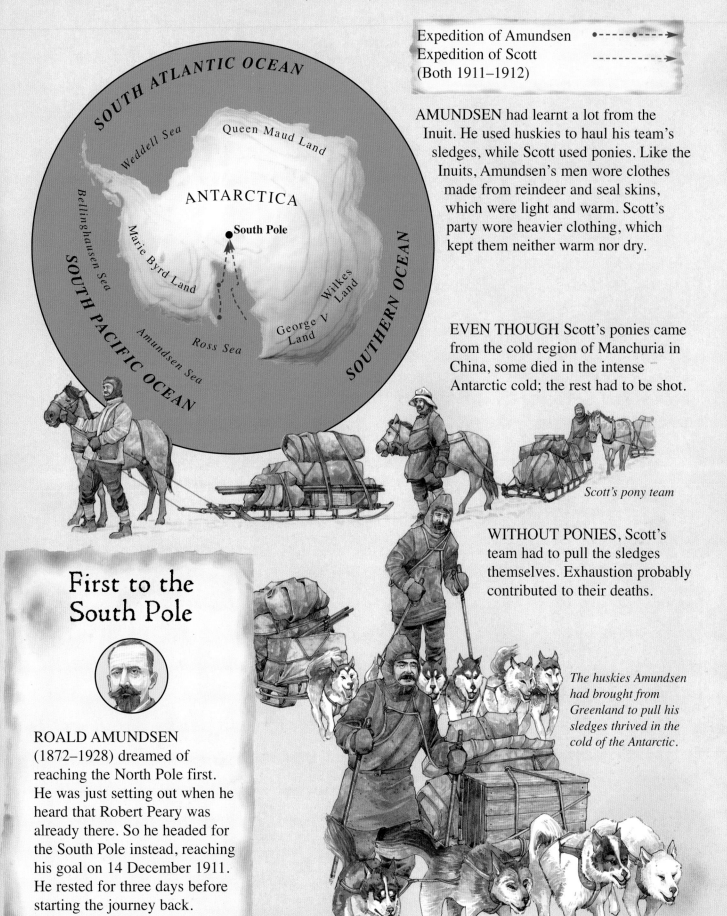

AMUNDSEN had learnt a lot from the Inuit. He used huskies to haul his team's sledges, while Scott used ponies. Like the Inuits, Amundsen's men wore clothes made from reindeer and seal skins, which were light and warm. Scott's party wore heavier clothing, which kept them neither warm nor dry.

EVEN THOUGH Scott's ponies came from the cold region of Manchuria in China, some died in the intense Antarctic cold; the rest had to be shot.

Scott's pony team

WITHOUT PONIES, Scott's team had to pull the sledges themselves. Exhaustion probably contributed to their deaths.

The huskies Amundsen had brought from Greenland to pull his sledges thrived in the cold of the Antarctic.

First to the South Pole

ROALD AMUNDSEN (1872–1928) dreamed of reaching the North Pole first. He was just setting out when he heard that Robert Peary was already there. So he headed for the South Pole instead, reaching his goal on 14 December 1911. He rested for three days before starting the journey back.

BELOW THE WAVES

Early diving suit invented by August Siebe, 1819

AS MORE AND MORE of the Earth was explored, there remained one huge and almost unknown region. What lay below the world's oceans? The many myths about sea-monsters showed people's fascination for the undersea world – but they didn't have the technology to go there. The deepest oceans are difficult to explore: light cannot penetrate that far down, making it dark and cold. The water pressure is so great that without strong, reinforced hulls, deep-sea craft would be crushed.

Diving bell

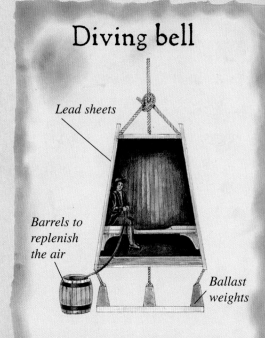

Lead sheets

Barrels to replenish the air

Ballast weights

SIR EDMUND HALLEY'S diving bell of 1690. Air trapped inside enabled men to work on the seabed.

The Alvin
A submersible for deep-sea research

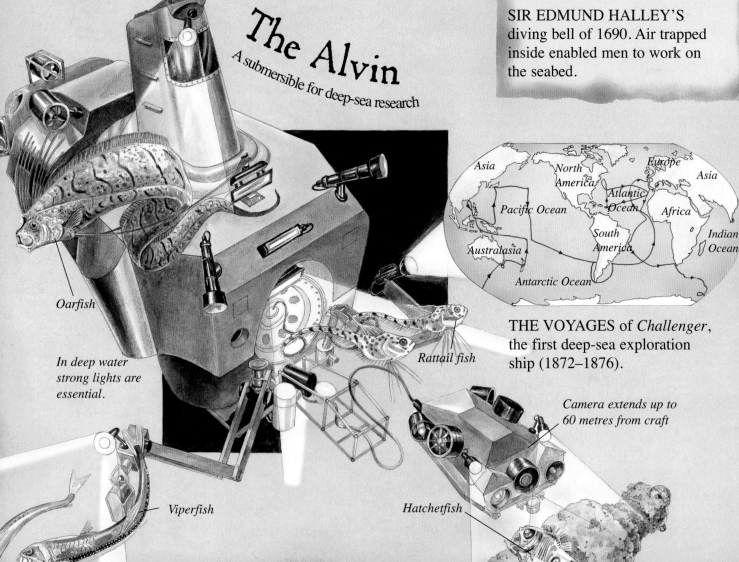

Oarfish

In deep water strong lights are essential.

Rattail fish

Asia
North America
Europe
Asia
Pacific Ocean
Atlantic Ocean
Africa
Indian Ocean
South America
Australasia
Antarctic Ocean

THE VOYAGES of *Challenger*, the first deep-sea exploration ship (1872–1876).

Camera extends up to 60 metres from craft

Viperfish

Hatchetfish

JACQUES COUSTEAU invented the aqualung in 1943. Cylinders of compressed air are strapped onto a diver's back. The air is breathed through a special valve. Another name for the device is 'scuba', which stands for **S**elf-**C**ontained **U**nderwater **B**reathing **A**pparatus.

Aqua-Lung™

The bathyscaphe

Bathyscaphe

THE BATHYSCAPHE was invented by Belgian explorer Auguste Picard.

PICARD'S *TRIESTE*, with its crew of two, took eight hours to reach the bottom of the Mariana Trench – the deepest spot on Earth at 11,000 metres – in 1960. The craft was subjected to immense pressure.

Spherical crew compartment

Extra-thick steel walls

Textile II, oil exploration vehicle

IN TODAY'S DIVING SUITS of strengthened metal, a diver can work about 200 metres below the sea's surface. Inside the suit the air pressure is normal. For deep diving, suits have been developed which allow for depths of up to 700m.

Mariana Trench

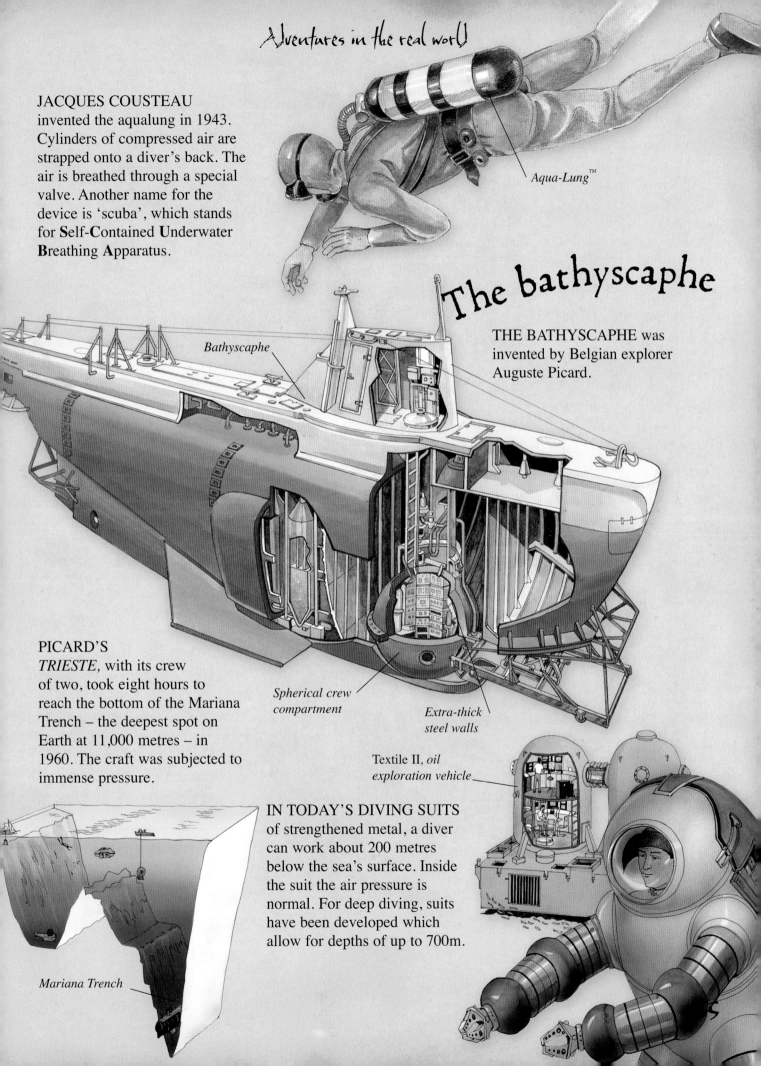

EXPLORING SPACE

Apollo 13

SPACE EXPLORATION is difficult because of the huge distances involved. Some planets are so far away that the light waves from them were first transmitted when dinosaurs still roamed the Earth! By the mid-20th century, new technology finally made space exploration possible. Scientists in America and the USSR had developed rocket technology – first used by Germany in World War Two – to blast spacecraft beyond the pull of the Earth's gravity.

First man in Space

YURI GAGARIN (1934–1968), a Soviet cosmonaut, became the first man in space, orbiting the Earth one and a half times in 1961.

Orbit

Craft lands

Gagarin lands

Re-entry

EARTH

Launch

Orbit

Moon landing 1969

> I'd better collect plenty of moon rock – who knows if we'll be back?

Spacecraft

Rocket

The Vostok rocket that blasted Gagarin into space was over 30 metres high.

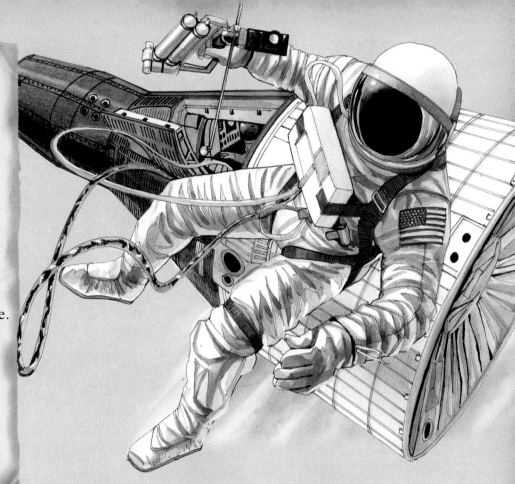

'One giant leap for mankind'

IN 1961 American President John F. Kennedy declared his commitment to land a man on the Moon within the next decade. In 1969 this became reality, and television viewers around the world watched Neil Armstrong and Buzz Aldrin walk on the Moon's surface.

THE FIRST lunar missions were called *Apollo* after the Greek god who was the guardian of travellers.

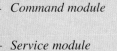

Command module

Service module

Lunar module

Third stage

Second stage

First stage

The Saturn rocket that took the Apollo Moon expedition into space in 1969.

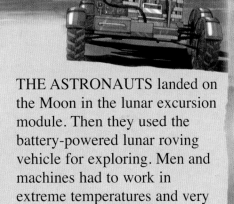

THE ASTRONAUTS landed on the Moon in the lunar excursion module. Then they used the battery-powered lunar roving vehicle for exploring. Men and machines had to work in extreme temperatures and very low gravity.

Shuttles

SPACE EXPLORATION is enormously expensive. To reduce the costs, the Space Shuttle, a reusable spacecraft, was designed. It is taken into space by a pair of booster rockets. Once in space it uses small rocket motors. When back in the Earth's gravity, it flies like a glider.

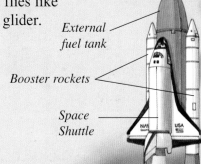

External fuel tank

Booster rockets

Space Shuttle

57

ROBOTS TO MARS!

Mars Pathfinder

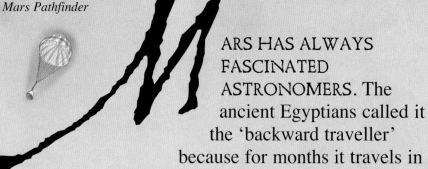

MARS HAS ALWAYS FASCINATED ASTRONOMERS. The ancient Egyptians called it the 'backward traveller' because for months it travels in one direction and then suddenly appears to travel backwards. The Romans called it Mars after their god of war.

Early telescopes were not very powerful, which led to many incorrect ideas about the planet's surface, including the belief that it was criss-crossed by irrigation canals. *Mars Global Surveyor* was launched in 1996 to carry out a long-term study from an orbit around the planet. In its first three years, MGS returned more data that all previous Mars missions combined, including high-resolution images of the so-called 'face on Mars'.

MARINER 9 orbited Mars every 12 hours for nearly a year in 1971. It sent back pictures showing a dust storm covering the entire planet. When the storm ended the craters of four huge volcanoes were visible.

Viking probes 1975

ONLY ROBOTS can explore Mars – no human could survive there without specially developed suits. In 1975 two *Viking* probes (right) landed on the planet. They collected rocks and sent back colour pictures, but found no signs of life.

IN 1971 the USSR's *Mars 3* captured the first panorama of the planet's surface. But it was photographs taken by the American *Mariner 9* during 1971 and 1972 that gave the first really clear information about the planet's surface.

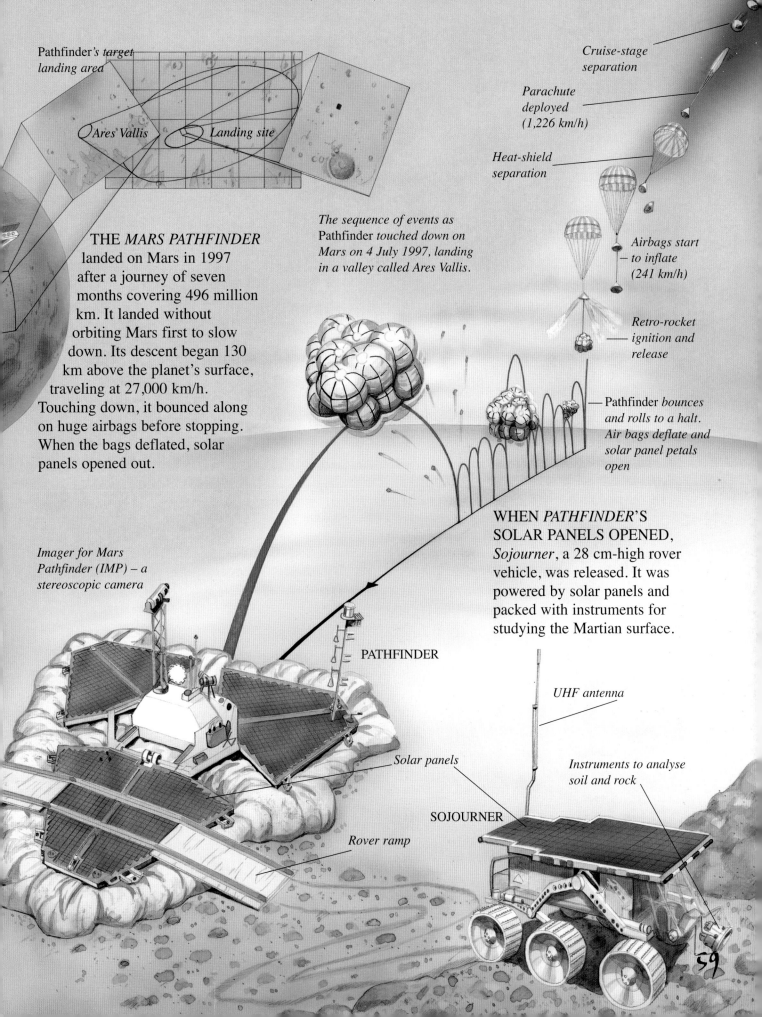

Pathfinder's target landing area

Ares Vallis   Landing site

Cruise-stage separation

Parachute deployed (1,226 km/h)

Heat-shield separation

The sequence of events as Pathfinder touched down on Mars on 4 July 1997, landing in a valley called Ares Vallis.

Airbags start to inflate (241 km/h)

Retro-rocket ignition and release

Pathfinder bounces and rolls to a halt. Air bags deflate and solar panel petals open

THE *MARS PATHFINDER* landed on Mars in 1997 after a journey of seven months covering 496 million km. It landed without orbiting Mars first to slow down. Its descent began 130 km above the planet's surface, traveling at 27,000 km/h. Touching down, it bounced along on huge airbags before stopping. When the bags deflated, solar panels opened out.

WHEN *PATHFINDER*'S SOLAR PANELS OPENED, *Sojourner*, a 28 cm-high rover vehicle, was released. It was powered by solar panels and packed with instruments for studying the Martian surface.

Imager for Mars Pathfinder (IMP) – a stereoscopic camera

PATHFINDER

UHF antenna

Solar panels

Instruments to analyse soil and rock

SOJOURNER

Rover ramp

59

A FUTURE IN SPACE?

Artist's impression of a spacecraft landing on Mars

SURPRISINGLY, THE REAL PROBLEM with space exploration lies not with technology, but cost.

Exploring with probes and other robots is useful, but limited. Humans make the best explorers, but at present they cannot survive conditions on Mars, the planet likely to be explored first.

However, travel to the Moon once seemed beyond the realms of possibility too, so perhaps humans will be able to explore further in the future.

TRAVELLING TO Mars would take at least six months – manned spacecraft are heavier than robot probes.

Astronauts will explore in a rover vehicle like this

The huge distance to travel here means that we will be away from Earth for at least three years.

SCOTT

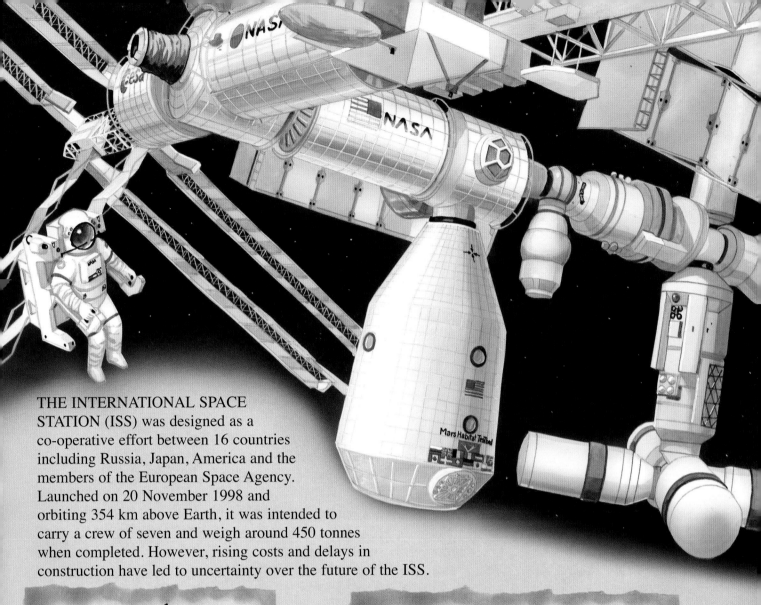

THE INTERNATIONAL SPACE STATION (ISS) was designed as a co-operative effort between 16 countries including Russia, Japan, America and the members of the European Space Agency. Launched on 20 November 1998 and orbiting 354 km above Earth, it was intended to carry a crew of seven and weigh around 450 tonnes when completed. However, rising costs and delays in construction have led to uncertainty over the future of the ISS.

Space colonies

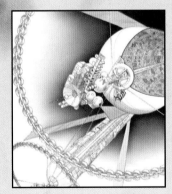

IN THE 1970s American scientists began to design a space colony that could replicate conditions on Earth. It would have gravity, seasons, plants and water, and could be used if Earth became uninhabitable.

Living in space

THE BIGGEST challenge for astronauts is staying alive. Once on Mars, they would need to stay there until its orbit aligned with Earth's again – which happens every 18 to 24 months. Research on living in space is already underway at the Johnson Space Center, Texas. A Mars Habitat Testbed Module is part of the International Space Station, and will provide a better understanding of long-term space travel.

GLOSSARY

Akkadians people from Akkad, a kingdom which flourished around 3500 BC in what is now Iraq.

align to be in line; used to refer to the position of planets.

archaeologist a person who studies human history by looking at the physical remains of the past.

arid very dry and unsuitable for growing plants.

Assyria the state which dominated much of what is now Iraq from about 1500 to 650 BC.

astronomer a scientist who studies space and the objects in it, such as planets.

bilge the lowest part of a ship's hull.

barbarian an uncultured, uncivilised person.

cartographer a person who draws maps.

conquistadors military commanders sent by the rulers of Spain to conquer America (the 'New World').

embalming a way of preserving dead bodies.

evolve to change over a long period of time and become better suited to your surroundings.

fossils preserved remains of ancient living things.

incense perfume burned during religious ceremonies.

irrigation an artificial method of taking water to fields and crops.

isthmus a narrow strip of land joining two larger areas.

khan ruler of the Mongols.

longships the Vikings' long, narrow warships, powered by oarsmen and sails.

Low Countries the region of north-west Europe covering modern Belgium, the Netherlands and Luxembourg.

Middle Ages a period of European history, roughly from 1000 to 1453.

Mongols nomadic people who lived in Central Asia.

myrrh a strong-smelling resin obtained from trees, used to make perfumes.

mythical not really existing, except in myths and legends.

orbit the regular path taken by one object around another. For example, the Earth orbits the Sun.

Ottomans the powerful rulers of the Turkish empire between the 15th and 19th centuries.

pack animal an animal that carries goods on its back.

prow the front of a boat.

silt very fine earth carried by a river. When the river slows, or floods, the silt is deposited on the ground or the riverbed.

source the place where a river begins.

Soviet coming from the USSR.

Spanish Main the area of land and sea in and around the Caribbean which was controlled by Spain in the 16th century.

stockade a strong defensive fence, usually wooden, around a homestead or fort.

strait a narrow stretch of sea linking two larger seas.

USSR (Union of Soviet Socialist Republics) a group of countries once ruled as a single state by the Russian government in Moscow. Most of these countries are now known officially as the Commonwealth of Independent States.

visiting card a small card printed with a person's name and address. In Victorian and Edwardian times middle and upper-class people left a card if they visited someone but found they were not at home.

INDEX